Hodder & Stoughton

A MEMBER OF THE HODDER HEADLINE GROUP

Acknowledgements

Photos: p. 7 © PA Photos; p. 9 © EPA/PA Photos

Illustrations: Pete Smith

Every effort has been made to trace copyright holders of material reproduced in this book. Any rights not acknowledged will be acknowledged in subsequent printings if notice is given to the publisher.

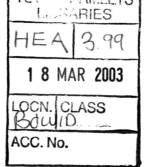
Orders; please contact Bookpoint Ltd, 130 Milton Park, Abingdon, Oxon OX14 4SB. Telephone (44) 01235 827720, Fax: (44) 01235 400454. Lines are open from 9.00–6.00, Monday to Saturday, with a 24 hour message answering service. You can also order through our website www.hodderheadline.co.uk

British Library Cataloguing in Publication Data
A catalogue record for this title is available from the British Library

ISBN 0 340 87307 8

First published 2003
Impression number   10 9 8 7 6 5 4 3 2 1
Year   2007 2206 2005 2004 2003

Copyright © John Townsend 2003

Typeset by SX Composing DTP, Rayleigh, Essex.
Printed in Great Britain for Hodder & Stoughton Educational, a division of Hodder Headline, 338 Euston Road, London NW1 3BH by The Bath Press Ltd, Bath.

Contents

1 Cops and Robbers

Crime is big news.
Papers are full of it.
They always have been.
Cops and robbers make good stories.
After all, crime happens all the time.
It's going on right now.
Somewhere.
Robbers are always at work.
Often in broad daylight.

Even so, most robbers do get caught in time.
Many live to regret what they do.
A lot end up saying that crime doesn't pay.
Not in the long run.
Not when they have to keep on the look-out.
Not when they end up behind bars.

The world is full of people who dream
of getting rich quick.
Some see crime as the only way
to get their hands on cash.
It's always been that way.
Ever since the first robber shouted
'Hand it over!'

Robbery is serious crime.
With theft it's the most common
crime in Britain.
Robbery is more than theft.
Robbers use force – or the fear of force.
Their victims get hurt.
They can be in real danger.
Some have to live with the terror for years.
All because of greed.
Greed that makes someone attack.

But you'll see how it doesn't always work.
You'll find proof that
robbers don't tend to live *happy ever after*.

The news tells stories every day of robbers
who try to rob tills in shops.
Or if a gang holds up a bank.
Or if a robber in a mask
runs into a post office.
They may end up on video.
You may see them on *Crimewatch*.
They're unlikely to get far.

Now and again a big story hits the news.
That's when a gang goes for the big prize.
When nothing will stop the real crooks.
A gang that hits the big time.
Robbery with teeth.

2 The Great Train Robbery

It wasn't daylight robbery.
But it was robbery all right.
It was one of the big crimes
of the twentieth century.

At 3 a.m. on 8 August 1963,
a gang held up the mail train.
It was on its way from Glasgow to London.
Men stole 120 mail bags full of money.
That was £2.6 million.
In 1963 that was huge money.
It was the biggest train robbery ever.

The gang planned the attack for months.
Over 12 men were in the gang.
They cut phone wires.
They made a hide-out in an empty farm house.
They fixed the rail signals.
They put a glove over the green light.
Then they shone a red light as the train came.
It was an empty spot 40 miles north of London.

When the train came to a stop,
the gang jumped on.
They hit the driver with iron bars.
One of the gang took the controls.
He drove the train to a road bridge.
They left the rear seven cars behind.
Many workers were sorting the mail inside.
They had no idea what was going on.

Now the gang could unload the sacks of cash.
It all went to plan,
but the train driver was hurt.
His name was Jack Mills.
He never got over that blow to his head.

It took just 15 minutes.
With the front of the train
now on a bridge over a road,
the gang threw down sacks
to the trucks below.
They had to be fast.
The alarm could go at any time.
They left some of the sacks behind
and sped off in the waiting trucks.

Now the gang had to lie low
until all the fuss died down.
At last they made a run for it.
They all took their share of the money.
The plan was to burn down the farm
to get rid of any clues.
It went wrong.
The men hired to clean up didn't do their job.
When the police found the farm
they also found lots of clues.
There were fingerprints.
Lots of them.

The police got to work.
In a year they had half of the robbers.
They were sent to prison for 30 years.
Soon the rest of the gang was behind bars.
It looked like it was all over.

Leatherslade Farm, where the gang hid after the 'Great Train Robbery' .

In the end,
most of the gang left prison after 12 years.
Only ten per cent of their hoard was found.
It seemed as if it was all worth it.
Or was it?
Did they really get away with it?
Not really.
Each of the gang got a share of the cash,
but for all their years in prison,
they could have earned far more in a real job.
For Ronnie Biggs it was far from a happy end.
Was it really all worth it?

3 The Brink's-Mat Job

It was November 1983.
A gang was waiting.
They had their eyes on a warehouse
at Heathrow Airport.
Unit 7 was like a huge safe.
Full of nice things.
A firm called Brink's-Mat kept
gold, jewels and art locked inside.
Six armed men wanted the lot.

A guard turned up for work at 6.30 p.m.
He was late.
The alarm was turned off to let him in.
That's when the gang struck.
They ran in wearing masks.
They had guns.
They got hold of all the guards and tied them up,
but how could they get into the main safe?

The gang got a petrol can.
They tipped it over one of the guards.
If he didn't tell them how to get in the safe,
they'd strike a match.
They soon got what they wanted.

In 15 minutes the gang had filled their van.
They'd loaded it with 3 tons of gold.
It was worth over £26 million.
That's ten times more than
'The Great Train Robbery'.
That was 20 years earlier.
Now the Brink's-Mat job
was the biggest robbery in Britain.
It still is.

The police soon got to work.
They spoke to all the guards.
How had the gang got in?
There was something fishy about one of them.
The one who was late that night.
The gang had known just when to strike.
Did they have inside help?
The guard began to talk.
His brother-in-law was a well-known crook.
The police soon knew who they were after.

The gang couldn't hide for long.
The police were on to them.
The net closed in.
A few of the robbers were soon behind bars.
Two of them went to prison for 25 years each.
Now the police had to mop up the rest.
They kept watch on a house in Kent.
At last it was time for a raid.
There was quite a fight.
One of the police was stabbed.
But the last of the robbers were caught.

The gang and their helpers went to prison.
The police found a lot of the missing gold.
The case of the Brink's-Mat Job
went into the history books.
It had been a daring raid.
The gang was mean and tough.
The robbers were brutal.
But it didn't do them much good.
Not in the end.
It wasn't worth the effort!

4   Closer to Home

The police had a problem.
A gang of robbers was on the loose.
By 1997 there had been 24 raids.
All the same.
Not on banks or shops,
but on homes near London.
All were close to motorways.
What was worse, the robbers were violent.
Each raid was well planned.
The gang didn't waste time.
It was quick – and brutal.

The raids were all the same.
The gang would strike when
people were at home.
They wore masks.
They had guns and iron bars.
They would smash their way in and attack.
Sometimes they beat their victims.

The gang used force to find out
where money and jewels were.
As the gang liked to take 'up-market' goods,
the police called them the 'Hob-Nob Gang'.
Thieves often refer to rich targets as 'hob-nobs'.

The robbers had no class about them.
They hit one man with a bat and yelled,
'You'll never look the same again'.
Even old people or small children
were tied up.
The gang used handcuffs.
Twice they shot pet dogs that barked.
The police just had to stop them.
If not, they knew robbery
could soon turn to murder.

The police went through all their files.
They checked all the names they knew.
They kept an eye on all suspects.
They spoke to anyone
who would sell any secrets.
At last there were two names on the list.
Two men who lived nearby.
The police kept watch on them in pubs
or on the street.

Soon there were three suspects.
One of them was seen putting a bag
in a rubbish bin in a car park.

When police looked in the bag, they saw
a pillowcase and four pairs of trainers.
That was odd.
They took them away for tests.
Then news came in of a raid the day before.
A gang of four masked men had stolen £20,000
from a house in north west London.
There were no footprints at the scene.
There was no link to the trainers.
It was the pillowcase that did the trick.
It came from the house that was robbed.
There was no doubt.

The police couldn't act yet.
The suspect would say
he'd found the pillowcase.
There had to be more proof.
The police had to keep under cover.
They already knew the man
had a stolen car.
It was a Volvo.
They saw him stop to pick up five men.

They were sure this was the gang,
but they had to catch them red-handed.
Only then could there be proof
to lock them away.

The Volvo pulled into a golf club car park.
The men got out.
The police kept at a distance,
but they felt sure a raid was about to start.
They called for extra police to come
in unmarked cars.

Not far away a family was at home.
Mrs. Burke turned off the TV.
She picked up her three year-old girl.
'Time for bed.'

Suddenly four men burst into the room.
They were in black and wore masks.
'Where's the safe?' they yelled.

'We haven't got one!' she cried.
The little girl screamed.

'Then we'll have your watch.
Get that ring off, too.'

The gang grabbed Mr. Burke in the next room.
'Tell us where the safe is or we'll kill him.
Then we'll take the kid.'

Mrs. Burke begged them.
'I told you. We haven't got a safe.'

Out came the handcuffs.
The three of them were handcuffed
to the stair rails.
The gang scooped up any jewels
they could find.
They grabbed a pillowcase and filled it.
In ten minutes they'd gone.

When the gang got back in the Volvo
the police were ready.
All six were caught red handed.
They had cash, handcuffs,
jewels in a pillowcase,
two-way radios, masks – the lot.

The Burke family was soon set free.
They were safe.
They got their things back.

With the arrest of the six men,
the raids stopped.
Homes in the area were safe again.

At the end of 1997,
the gang of six went to court.
They were all found guilty.
The two ring-leaders were sent to prison
for 18 years each.
The rest got between 12 and 15 years
behind bars.
The 'Hob-Nob Gang' no longer
had stolen goods on their hands.
Just time.

5 'You're Nicked'

Some robbers get away with it – most don't.
Some get more than they thought.
Some robbers seem to make the most
stupid mistakes.
Here are a few recent stories from the news.
They are all true.
They all go to show that crime can be
a bad choice of career.

Robber fired
James Elliot went to rob a man in California.
He pointed his gun at his victim
and pulled the trigger.
The gun didn't go off.
What did he do?
He looked down the end and tried again.
This time the gun worked.
End of robbery!

Putting a foot in it

A robber in the USA had a bright idea.

He didn't want to leave any fingerprints.

So what did he do?

He took off his socks

and put them over his hands.

A few days later he was arrested.

Why?

The police got him by tracing his toe prints.

Photo-fit

Another robber in the USA made a blunder.
He found a camera in the house he was robbing.
He picked it up –
it wasn't worth taking.
He put it down again.
Click.
He didn't know he'd taken his own photo.
When the police came,
they looked at the camera.
They saw the photo.
Guess what?
They found the robber with no trouble at all.

Plane silly

There's nothing like highway robbery.
This was just high robbery.
A man called Augusto got on a plane
going to Manila.
It was May 2000.
He had plans.
Suddenly, he put on a ski mask and goggles.
He pulled out a gun and a grenade.
He went round the plane
and robbed people of about $25,000.
He told the pilot to lower the plane
to 1,000 metres.
The pilot did as he was told.

Augusto tied a home-made parachute to his back.

He opened the door.

The wind was very strong.

It blew him over.

Someone gave him a kick and out he went.

Just before he fell out,

he took the pin out of the grenade.

He would get his own back.

The trouble was, he threw the pin into the plane

and kept hold of the grenade.

No one saw Augusto again.

Nor his stolen money.

But they heard the grenade.

He didn't quite make it as a robber.

6 Do Sleep Well

A few crime stories don't quite make it
onto *Crimewatch*.
That's because the crimes solve themselves.
Here are three stories from the papers
from the last three years.
They may not be daylight robbery.
They may not hit the big time.
But they all go to show that crime
can have a funny side.

Guns and roses

November 2000.
Police sent roses to a couple to say 'sorry'.
Armed police had bundled Fred Martin (63)
and his wife Jane
out of their bed in the early hours.
The shocked couple were marched out
into the street in their night clothes.

Police were after a gunman.
A robber was on the loose.
There had been a raid in South London.
The gunman was nowhere to be seen.
The police had been given the wrong address.
Oops!

A fair cop
June 2001.
The police stopped a driver in Durham.
They were looking for a robber.
A man ran from the car
to make a getaway.
He raced to jump in a taxi.
But it didn't speed him away.
He sat in the back as it went nowhere.
It was the police car!
He wasn't a robber at all – just drunk.
One officer said, 'I laughed so much
I could hardly put the cuffs on him'.
Gary McGowan was fined £300
and banned from driving for 18 months.

Bingo Women Beat Off Gang

October 2002.
Four masked robbers armed with a crowbar
ran into a bingo hall in Bradford.
They tried to get the takings from the till.

Two old age pensioners
weren't going to let robbers
spoil their bingo.

The two old ladies set about the gang
with a walking stick and an umbrella.
They hit the men round their heads.
The robbers backed away
from the nagging women.
They gave up and ran off.
They didn't get a penny.
One of the women later said,
'I don't know what came over me.
I just got so mad.'
No one knows what the robbers later said!

Perhaps it's a safer world after all.
Maybe robbers don't get away so easily.

The ones behind bars
have lost a lot of years.
All freedom gone.
Nothing less than daylight robbery!

As they say on *Crimewatch* . . .
'Don't have nightmares.
Do sleep well.'

Sweet dreams!